BLACK

THE AMERICAN BLACK IN AVIATION

WINGS

BY VON HARDESTY AND DOMINICK PISANO

Published by the

NATIONAL AIR AND SPACE MUSEUM

SMITHSONIAN INSTITUTION

Distributed by

SMITHSONIAN INSTITUTION PRESS

Washington, D.C.

INTRODUCTION

Von Hardesty and Dominick Pisano

Copyright © 1983 National Air and Space Museum

Library of Congress Cataloging in Publication Data

Hardesty, Von, 1939-
  Black wings.

  Bibliography: p.
  1. Afro-Americans in aeronautics —
     United States.
  I. Pisano, Dominick, 1943-
  II. National Air and Space Museum.
  III. Title.
TL553.H34
1983   387.7′08996073   83-2404

ISBN 0-87474-511-X
10 9 8 7 6 5 4

Book Design by
Gerard A. Valerio, Bookmark Studio, Inc.

First edition produced by the Office of Public Affairs and Museum Services, National Air and Space Museum
Publications Coordinator: Helen C. McMahon

Cover Photograph: Harold Hurd, 1936, Challenger Air Pilots' Association, Chicago.
(Harold Hurd)

At first glance, the term "black aviation" appears artificial or even unhistorical. Some might suggest that the language stems from a contemporary desire to identify the contributions of a minority to an important area of human endeavor. The use of the term black aviation, however, derives from history itself. Its usage in aeronautical history is inevitable and obligatory, a reflection of the fact that for the first half century of powered flight, blacks flew in largely segregated circumstances. Racial exclusion in aviation — as in other areas of life — mirrored the prevailing norms of American society.

Richard Wright portrayed this historical reality in his novel, *Native Son*, published in 1940. Wright describes two black youths watching in awe and frustration as an airplane performs intricate skywriting maneuvers above them. "I could fly a plane if I had a chance," one youth remarks confidently. His companion's response expresses poignantly the obstacles faced by blacks during these early years. "If you wasn't black and if you had some money and if they'd let you go to that aviation school, you could fly a plane."

The story of black aviation is one of breakthroughs against this restrictive social backdrop. At first there were isolated pioneers such as Bessie Coleman whose burning desire to fly overcame the entrenched racial discrimination of the time. Coleman's brief career as a stunt pilot provided inspiration for a generation of black youth who shared her enthusiasm for the airplane. By the time of Charles Lindbergh's flight to Paris in 1927, blacks had broken into aviation only in small numbers and struggled in isolation against the strong headwinds of racial prejudice.

To broaden black participation in the growing aeronautical world of the 1930s, flying clubs were organized. William J. Powell in Los Angeles and Cornelius R. Coffey in Chicago provided leadership for these crucial endeavors. Powell set up the Bessie Coleman Aero Clubs on the West Coast, wrote his visionary book, *Black Wings*, and appealed to black youth to enter aviation as a career field. Affirming similar goals, Coffey ran his own school of aeronautics and served as the first president of the National Airmen's Association. Both men saw clearly that blacks needed technical skills, not individual exploits in barnstorming, to establish their place in aviation.

The long-distance flights of C. Alfred Anderson and Dr. Albert E. Forsythe in 1933 and 1934 demonstrated the growing competence of black fliers. By making dramatic flights across America, to Canada, and to the Caribbean, Anderson and Forsythe displayed their flying skill even as they appealed for full equality in the field of aviation. The Anderson-Forsythe team also took pains to plan their flights well, mobilizing the black press, enlisting the aid of the National Urban League and christening one of their aircraft with the historic name, the "Spirit of Booker T. Washington." Both fliers identified their achievements with the broader aims of racial harmony.

The federal government provided an impetus for change when Congress established the Civilian Pilot Training Program in 1939. For the first time, blacks were given access to federally-funded flight training and were formally recognized as participants in the growing field of aviation. Despite the modest funds allocated for the segregated black training program, the number of licensed black pilots grew dramatically.

Yet flying in the late 1930s presented familiar frustrations for blacks: hostile and unpredictable receptions at established airfields, segregated facilities, the refusal of some airports to service aircraft flown by blacks and the feeling of alienation from the aviation community as a whole. Although the Civilian Pilot Training Program trained blacks in significant numbers, the total effect, ironically, was to multiply the frustrations already felt by black pilots.

When the United States Army Air Corps activated the 99th Fighter Squad-

ron in March 1941, blacks achieved their first tenuous foothold in the sphere of military aviation. Civil rights leaders such as Walter White and A. Philip Randolph had long advocated the admission of blacks into the elite ranks of the Air Corps on an integrated basis, but the War Department and the Air Corps resisted the idea. As a result, when black cadets trained at the newly-established Tuskegee Army Air Field on the eve of Pearl Harbor, they flew as part of what could only be described as a separate black air force.

Between 1941 and 1945, the "Tuskegee Experiment," as the training of black fighter pilots became known, was proof that blacks in great numbers could be trained and mobilized for the sophisticated task of combat flying. In the air war over Europe, the 99th Fighter Squadron joined three other all-black fighter units to compose the 332d Fighter Group. Together, these units demonstrated that the Tuskegee Experiment had been a success. Colonel Benjamin O. Davis, Jr., Commander of the 332d, wisely stressed professionalism and combat efficiency. His effective leadership did much to erode the hostility to black participation in military aviation. Black airmen returned from the war with a keen sense of accomplishment which was equaled only by their impatience with the existing pattern of racial segregation.

The Tuskegee airmen had dispelled the myth that blacks could not master the technical skills associated with combat flying. At the same time, the war years exposed the costs, both human and material, of maintaining separate black air units. Wartime segregation had proven to be unwieldy, inefficient and expensive. With the demonstration of black capability in military aviation came a transformation in national policy. In 1948, President Harry S Truman's Executive Order 9981 called for equal opportunity in the armed forces. In 1949, the United States Air Force became the first armed service to implement this historic change in direction. On a less formal basis in the post-war years, the civilian sphere of aviation slowly began to reflect the goal of integration. By the 1960s, blacks, benefiting from gains realized in military aviation and the wave of civil rights legislation, began to appear in commercial aviation in positions of responsibility. In the 1970s, blacks entered the ranks of the astronaut program.

In the present decade, blacks are involved in many areas of the aerospace community. Moreover, their contributions to aeronautical history in the United States are finally being documented and recognized after years of historical neglect. In view of the record of black struggle and achievement in aviation, the National Air and Space Museum is pleased to add this pictorial history to the growing collection of scholarship in black studies.

HEADWINDS

The historic flight of the Wright brothers in 1903 sparked a popular enthusiasm for aviation. Participation by black Americans in the new age of flight, however, did not come easily. Racial discrimination, at the time still deeply embedded in American life, stood as a powerful barrier to any vision of "black wings."

There was the widely-held notion in the aviation community that blacks lacked even the aptitude to fly. Blacks found themselves arbitrarily excluded from flight instruction. Faced with racial exclusion at home, Eugene Bullard and Bessie Coleman, the first black Americans to become licensed pilots, obtained their pilot training in France.

During the decade after Charles Lindbergh's 1927 flight across the Atlantic, blacks began to break into aviation. Flying clubs appeared in Chicago and Los Angeles. These active centers of black aviation promoted airmindedness, organized air shows and sponsored long-distance flights.

By 1941, many of the old stereotypes had been shattered. Segregation persisted, but the number of licensed black pilots had reached 102, a tenfold increase in one decade. Black Americans had demonstrated their keen interest in flight and the desire to participate on a basis of full equality in civil and military aviation.

1. Grover C. Nash became the first black to fly the air mail during National Air Mail Week in 1938. Nash flew an intrastate route from Chicago to Mattoon to Charleston, Illinois. (Harold Hurd)

Pioneers

Two important breakthroughs set the stage for blacks to enter the field of aviation. Eugene Bullard earned his wings as a pilot with the French during World War I. At home, Bessie Coleman of Chicago broke into aviation as a stunt pilot in the early 1920s.

2.

4.

2, 3. In 1922, Bessie Coleman became the first licensed black pilot in the United States. After her flight training in France, she returned to America to pursue a career as a barnstormer. She died in 1926 at the age of 33 in an aircraft accident. Her brief flying career inspired many young blacks to enter the field of aviation.

4. Born in Columbus, Georgia, in 1894, Eugene Bullard served as an infantryman with the French Foreign Legion in World War I. In 1917, Bullard flew briefly with the French on the Western Front. (U.S. Air Force)

3.

Flying in Los Angeles

Los Angeles became an important center for black aviation. As early as 1929, a small group of aviation enthusiasts led by William J. Powell organized the Bessie Coleman Aero Clubs to promote airmindedness in the black community. On Labor Day, 1931, the flying club sponsored the first all-black air show in the United States, an event which attracted an estimated 15,000 spectators. Through the Bessie Coleman School, the number of black aviators increased dramatically despite the economic hardships of the Depression.

5.

William J. Powell published *Black Wings* in 1934. (6.) Dedicated to Bessie Coleman, the book appealed to black men and women "to fill the air with black wings." A visionary proponent of aviation, Powell urged black youth to carve out their own destiny—to become pilots, aircraft designers and business leaders in the field of aviation. To the Depression era generation, he offered the prospect of new jobs and a transportation system free of racial discrimination. The publicity flyer for *Black Wings* suggests Powell's optimism for future black involvement in aviation.

5. One of America's first black pilots, William J. Powell, president of the Bessie Coleman Aero Clubs, actively promoted aviation in the black community. (*Northrop University*)

6.

7. Heavyweight boxing champion Joe Louis (*second from left*) visits William J. Powell (*right*) at the workshop of the Bessie Coleman Aero Club in Los Angeles. (*Northrop University*)

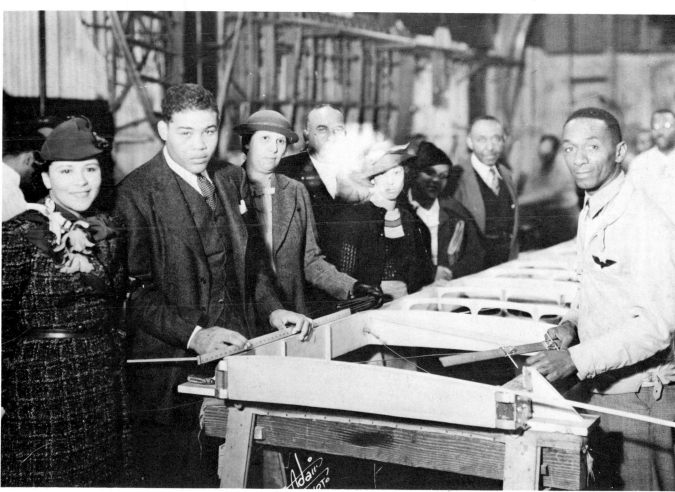

7.

8. Hubert Julian points to a billboard announcing his appearance in the 1931 Los Angeles black air show. One of the first licensed black pilots, Julian pursued a controversial career as a showman and promoter of black aviation. The billboard incorrectly refers to him as "Rupert" Julian. *(Northrop University)*

8.

9.

9. Powell appealed to black youth to take their place in the world of aviation. The March 1937 issue of *Craftsmen Aero News*, Powell's short-lived trade journal, portrayed the dream of flight and black youth. *(Schomburg Center for Research in Black Culture, N.Y. Public Library)*

10. Black aviation in Los Angeles achieved its greatest fame with the 1932 transcontinental flight of James Herman Banning and Thomas C. Allen. For their flight across the continent —the first by black aviators—they obtained a used aircraft and set off with less than $100 for expenses. The "Flying Hobos," as they were affectionately known, completed the flight in a flying time of 41 hours, 27 minutes. *(Thomas C. Allen)*

8

10.

JAMES HERMAN BANNING, 1900-1933

As a youth in Oklahoma, James Herman Banning (11, 12.) dreamed of becoming a pilot. His interest in flying drew him first to Chicago in the early 1920s, where he sought to enter an aviation school. No school would admit him because of his race — despite his aptitude for flying and two years at Iowa State University.

Rather than abandon his goal, Banning migrated to Des Moines, Iowa, where an army officer, Lt. Raymond Fischer, taught him to fly. When Banning moved to the West Coast in the late 1920s, he was one of a handful of black pilots licensed by the Department of Commerce.

Before Banning's tragic death in an airplane crash in 1933 (Banning was not at the controls), he had earned considerable attention as a stunt pilot. Banning's most memorable feat, however, was the 1932 transcontinental flight with his mechanic, Thomas C. Allen. *(M. Murlee Hart)*

11.

12.

13. Grover C. Nash of Chicago stands next to his Buhl Bull Pup monoplane. *(Harold Hurd)*

Flying in Chicago

Chicago rivaled Los Angeles as a center of black aviation. In 1931, the Challenger Air Pilots' Association, inspired by the legacy of Bessie Coleman, organized a small group of air enthusiasts to promote aviation in the black community. At Harlem Airport in the Depression years, the Coffey School of Aeronautics offered expert flight instruction. To provide a nationwide organization for black aviators, Chicago became the home of the National Airmen's Association in 1939.

14. The Curtiss-Wright Aeronautical School provided instruction in aircraft mechanics to its first all-black class in 1931. Cornelius R. Coffey *(right foreground)*, a certified airplane and engine mechanic, later established his own flight training school. *(Cornelius R. Coffey)*

15. The Challenger Air Pilots' Association became Chicago's first black flying club. Organized by John C. Robinson *(far right)*, the club built its first airstrip in the black township of Robbins, Illinois, in 1933. Blacks had been excluded from established airports in the Chicago area. *(Harold Hurd)*

14.

15.

"WILLA BROWN VISITS THE *CHICAGO DEFENDER*"

"When Willa Brown, a young woman wearing white jodhpurs, jacket and boots, strode into our newsroom in 1936, she made such a stunning appearance that all the typewriters, which had been clacking noisily, suddenly went silent. Unlike most first-time visitors, she wasn't at all bewildered. She had a confident bearing and there was an undercurrent of determination in her voice.

" 'I want to speak to Mr. Enoch Waters,' she said. I wasn't unhappy at the prospect of discovering who she was and what she wanted. I had an idea she was a model representing a new commercial product that she had been hired to promote. 'I'm Willa Brown,' she informed me, seating herself without being asked.

"In a businesslike manner she explained that she was an aviatrix and wanted some publicity for a Negro air show at Harlem Airport on the city's southwest side. Except for the colorful 'Colonel' Hubert Fauntleroy Julian, who called himself the 'Black Eagle' and who had gained a lot of publicity for his exploits, and 'Colonel' John Robinson, a Chicago flyer who was in Ethiopia heading up Haile Selassie's air force, I was unaware of any other Negro aviators, particularly in Chicago.

" 'There are about thirty of us,' she informed me, 'both men and women.' Most were students, she added, but several had obtained their licenses and one, Cornelius Coffey, was an expert aviation and engine mechanic who also held a commercial pilot's license and was a certified flight instructor. He was the leader of the group. She informed me that she held a limited commercial pilot's license.

"Fascinated both by her and the idea of Negro aviators, I decided to follow up the story myself. Accompanied by a photographer, I covered the air show. About 200 or 300 other spectators attended, attracted by the story in the *Defender*. So happy was Willa over our appearance that she offered to take me up for a free ride. She was piloting a Piper Cub, which seemed to me, accustomed as I was to commercial planes, to be a rather frail craft. It was a thrilling experience, and the maneuvers—figure eights, flipovers and stalls—were exhilarating, though momentarily frightening. I wasn't convinced of her competence until we landed smoothly."

—Enoch Waters,
City Editor, *Chicago Defender*

16. *(Schomburg Center for Research in Black Culture, N.Y. Public Library)*

17. A sudden windstorm destroyed the hangar at Robbins Airport shortly after it opened. The Challenger Air Pilots' Association then moved its flight operations to Harlem Airport near Chicago. *(Harold Hurd)*

17.

18. John C. Robinson, President of Chicago's Challenger Air Pilots' Association, advised Emperor Haile Selassie on building the Ethiopian Air Force in 1935. Robinson, shown next to a Junkers aircraft in Ethiopia, recruited a number of pilots and technicians in Chicago to join him. Before the plan could be realized, Italy invaded Ethiopia. Robinson narrowly escaped, but his efforts aroused considerable interest in the black community. *(Harold Hurd)*

19.

18.

19. Janet Waterford Bragg, a registered nurse, purchased the first aircraft for the Challenger Air Pilots' Association. She was active in the Challenger organization in the 1930s. *(Harold Hurd)*

21. Cornelius R. Coffey *(right)* and Willa Brown *(center)* promoted aviation in the black community through the Coffey School of Aeronautics. They are pictured here with Dr. A. Porter Davis at the National Airmen's Association Air Meet at Chicago's Harlem Airport in August 1939. *(Harold Hurd)*

20. Earl W. Renfroe, a Chicago dentist, earned his pilot's license in 1934 and his transport license two years later. He is pictured in the cockpit of his Travel Air in 1937. *(Earl W. Renfroe)*

20.

21.

Air Shows

Black stunt pilots and parachutists, backed by daredevil motorcycling on the ground, performed at numerous air shows in the 1930s. The onlookers, largely black, thrilled to the performances of Willie "Suicide" Jones and Dorothy Darby.

24. Chauncey E. Spencer *(center)* completes a successful parachute jump at Chicago's black air show in March 1939. *(Harold Hurd)*

22. Harold Hurd was a member of the first all-black class to graduate from the Curtiss-Wright Aeronautical School. He obtained his private pilot's license at Harlem Airport, and later served as a Sergeant Major in the U. S. Army Air Forces training program at Tuskegee Institute during World War II. *(Harold Hurd)*

24.

23. Pioneer aviator Willa Brown *(center)* poses with Perry Young and his mother Edith at Chicago's Harlem Airport in the late 1930s. Young went on to a full-time career in aviation, first as a civilian flight instructor at Tuskegee during World War II and later as a commercial helicopter pilot. *(Perry H. Young, Jr.)*

Air and Ground Show

Second Annual Colored Air and Ground Show

SUNDAY SEPT. 24th

at 2 p. m.

Featuring

Miss Dorothy Darby of Cleveland
America's Only Professional Girl Parachute Jumper

Major George Fisher

Veteran Daredevil of Chicago, in a sensational delayed parachute leap from a Giant Plane 10,000 feet up. **Airplane Ride & Stunt Flying**

Peter Consdorf of Mobile in a death-defying dash on a Motorcycle through a flaming wooden wall of fire.

Ray Bridgers of Chattanooga, daring aerial performer, and others
Thompson Brothers Balloon and Parachute Company

LOCATION: Westchester Airport, Hillside, Ill. Take Westchester Elevated train at Adams Street. Auto Route:- West on Roosevelt Road to Hillside, direct to Westchester Airport · Plenty Parking Space

Come Early Refreshments

Music By
Capt. CURRY'S CONCERT BAND M.O.G.U.S.A.
Note: In case of Rain, Event will be held Sun. October 1st

ADMISSION Adults **35c**
Children **10c**

(Harold Hurd)

MAMMOTH AIR-SHOW

SUNDAY, AUG. 28, 12:30 P.M.

SPECIAL FEATURE

WILLIE "SUICIDE" JONES

Greatest Colored Professional Parachute Jumper, Fifteen Years Record. Will Attempt to

BRING WORLD'S RECORD

for Delayed Parachute Jump, to America

Present World's Record for Delayed Parachute Jump is (Russia) 26,500 Feet, Opening Chute at 650 Feet From Ground

KEN HUNTER

of the famous Hunter Bros. Endurance Record Holders Arranged to Pilot his Ship for Willie Jones

MARKHAM AIR FIELD

167th and **So. Western Ave.**
Near Harvey, Ill.

AERIAL ACROBATICS, ROLLS, TURNS, SPINS, RIBBON CUTTING, CRAZY FLYING

ADDED

MOTORCYCLE ATTRACTIONS

THRILLS GALORE

LARGE PARKING AREA REFRESHMENTS ON GROUND Sight Seeing Rides on 29-Passenger Boeings

ADMISSION, FIFTY CENTS

Representatives of the Aeronautics Adm. and N.A.A. to be Present
For Information Call MAJOR SIMMONS, Phone Drex. 0058

(Harold Hurd)

The Anderson-Forsythe Flights

C. Alfred Anderson and Dr. Albert E. Forsythe occupy a special place in the history of aviation for their long-distance flights in 1933 and 1934. As black aviators, they demonstrated considerable skill at flying and popularizing aviation in the black community. In 1933, they flew from Atlantic City to Los Angeles and back, the first round trip transcontinental flight by black pilots. Another long-distance flight to Canada followed in the same year. During the course of their flights, the team worked with the National Urban League to promote black involvement in aviation during the difficult days of the Depression.

The Pan-American Goodwill Flight of 1934 established a new benchmark for the Anderson-Forsythe team. Well-planned and daring in scope, the long-distance flight

27. C. Alfred Anderson (*left*) and Dr. Albert E. Forsythe are shown together before their demonstration flights in 1933 and 1934. (*Albert E. Forsythe*)

25. Forsythe and Anderson consult their map near Wichita, Kansas, enroute to the West Coast on their 1933 round trip transcontinental flight. (*Albert E. Forsythe*)

26. Anderson and Forsythe are shown arriving in their Fairchild 24 "Pride of Atlantic City" at Los Angeles in July 1933 after completing the first leg of their round trip transcontinental flight. (*Albert E. Forsythe*)

For Your Inspection

THE

"Booker T. Washington"

THE NEW CHRISTENED

AIRPLANE

For The

SOUTH-AMERICAN GOODWILL FLIGHT

Flown By

Dr. A Forsythe & C. Alfred Anderson

Mon. Sept. 24, 1934

6 P. M.

AT

Practice Golf Course

Argile & Haverford Roads Ardmore, Pa.

ATTY. H. H. ROBB GUEST SPEAKER

Sponsored by The Main Line Branch of the Inter-Racial Goodwill Aviation Committee

Committee- Rev. James Scott Chairman
Joseph Littlejohn Margaret Greer Jos. Struthers
George Pleasant Wilbur Whitney

(*C. Alfred Anderson*)

28. For the Pan-American Goodwill Flight of 1934, the Anderson-Forsythe team christened their Lambert Monocoupe the "Spirit of Booker T. Washington," in honor of the noted black educator. President Robert R. Moton of Tuskegee Institute (*left*) and his wife (*second from right*) are shown with Anderson and Forsythe at the christening ceremonies. (*Albert E. Forsythe*)

16

28.

endeavored to promote interracial harmony and at the same time demonstrate the growing skills of black pilots.

The initial leg of their journey consisted of a flight from Miami to Nassau, the first ever by a land plane. Subsequent stops included Havana, Jamaica, Haiti, the Dominican Republic, Puerto Rico, the Virgin Islands, Grenada, Trinidad, and British Guiana (Guyana). On their return flight from Trinidad, the fliers damaged the "Spirit of Booker T. Washington" while taking off from an improvised airstrip. This mishap brought the Caribbean flight to an end.

Through their bold flying, the Anderson-Forsythe team attracted worldwide attention. In the Caribbean, the U.S. Department of State gave the team active and cordial support. At home, the flight provided the black community with a source of pride. Both Anderson and Forsythe hoped that the long-distance flight would inspire black youth to see in aviation a new avenue for advancement.

31.

29.

29. Anderson and Forsythe begin their 1934 Pan-American Goodwill Flight with a cheering send-off. *(Albert E. Forsythe)*

30. Residents of Nassau greet Anderson and Forsythe after their flight from Miami in 1934. The fliers displayed extraordinary skill, landing the "Spirit of Booker T. Washington" at night on a dirt road with automobile lights for illumination. *(C. Alfred Anderson)*.

31. Anderson and Forsythe are greeted by the governor of the Bahamas *(left)* on the occasion of their flight to the Caribbean in 1934. *(Albert E. Forsythe)*

30.

FLIGHT LINES

Many blacks had displayed a keen desire during the 1920s and 1930s to take to the air, but as in other aspects of American life, their dreams of wide-scale involvement in aviation were met with continued indifference or hostility. America's flight lines were off limits to blacks who sought flight training or careers in aviation.

By the end of the 1930s, the role of blacks in aviation changed abruptly, first in the civilian sphere and then in the military. The year 1939 was especially auspicious. In that year the National Airmen's Association, organized to broaden the base of black participation in aviation, was chartered in Chicago. Also in 1939, the Spencer-White flight from Chicago to Washington dramatized the goal of wider black involvement in the aeronautical community.

In addition, 1939 saw the admission of blacks into the Civilian Pilot Training Program (CPT), which was established by the Civil Aeronautics Authority to provide a pool of civilian pilots for wartime emergency. By including provisions for black participation at six black colleges in the eastern United States and two non-academic flying schools in the midwest, CPT made it possible for blacks to receive flight instruction on a wide scale.

In the military sphere, a series of legislative moves on the part of Congress made possible the activation of the all-black 99th Fighter Squadron on March 22, 1941, despite opposition on the part of the Army Air Corps and the War Department. Tuskegee Army Air Field, located at Tuskegee Institute in Alabama, became the training center not only for the 99th but for all black fighter pilots during World War II.

As the program of black military aviation expanded to include the all-black 332d Fighter Group and 447th Bombardment Group, additional training facilities were required and established at bases such as Selfridge Field, Michigan, Hondo Field, Texas, and Chanute Field, Illinois.

1. Linkwood Williams, civilian flight instructor, Tuskegee Army Air Field. *(James O. Plinton, Jr.)*

Spencer-White Flight

In May 1939, Dale L. White and Chauncey E. Spencer, under the auspices of the National Airmen's Association and the *Chicago Defender*, flew from Chicago to Washington, D.C. to dramatize the goal of wider black involvement in aviation. While in Washington, White and Spencer met with Edgar G. Brown, a well-known civil rights leader, and Senator Harry S Truman to promote their cause.

2.

2. On the completion of their 3,000 mile round trip flight from Chicago to Washington, D.C., in 1939, Dale L. White *(center)* and Chauncey E. Spencer *(second from right)* are greeted by National Airmen's Association President Cornelius R. Coffey *(second from left). (Harold Hurd)*

3. On a stopover at New York's Floyd Bennett Field in May 1939, Chauncey E. Spencer visits with his sister, Alroy Spencer Rivers. *(Harold Hurd)*

3.

Civilian Pilot Training

The Civilian Pilot Training Program (CPT), which after Pearl Harbor became the War Training Service Program (WTS), allowed blacks to participate in aviation on a much larger scale than had previously been known. Among the black colleges included were Tuskegee Institute, Howard University and Hampton Institute. The Coffey School of Aeronautics in Chicago also took part in the program.

CPT provided a pool of black flight instructors for Tuskegee Army Air Field, the center for black military aviation during World War II. During the course of the war, an estimated 2,000 black pilots received their wings through CPT or WTS. Nearly all of the black military aviators who took part in the war were graduates of these programs.

5.

4.

4. Dignitaries gather in front of the first CPT aircraft to be delivered to Tuskegee Institute in Alabama. At far left are George L. Washington, Director of the Division of Aeronautics, Tuskegee Institute, and Dr. Fred L. Patterson, the Institute's president. At center, wearing helmet and goggles, is C. Alfred Anderson, chief primary flight instructor. *(James O. Plinton, Jr.)*

5. A CPT instructor discusses a flight maneuver with a student at the Coffey School of Aeronautics in Chicago. In addition to being a breakthrough for blacks in aviation, CPT was a pioneering equal rights program that allowed both men and women to participate. *(Charles N. Smallwood)*

6. A CPT-sponsored class in aviation mechanics was offered as part of the Coffey School of Aeronautics curriculum at Chicago's Wendell Phillips High School in 1941. *(Earl Franklin)*

6.

7. A group of WTS students at the Coffey School of Aeronautics assemble near the tail section of Waco UPF-7 trainer to listen to their instructor explain a flight problem. *(Dicey Gibbs)*

8. Three cadets in the 1943 WTS program at the Coffey School of Aeronautics stand next to their Waco trainer. Left to right: Edward Gibbs, Henri Fletcher and Charles Smallwood. Gibbs later founded Negro Airmen International, an organization devoted to promoting black interests in aviation. *(Charles N. Smallwood)*

8.

9. CPT students service a Stearman PT-13 at Tuskegee Institute. *(Schomburg Center for Research in Black Culture, N.Y. Public Library)*

7.

9.

Tuskegee Army Air Field

Tuskegee Army Air Field became the focal point for the training of black military pilots during World War II. Primary training of the first flying cadets began on July 19, 1941, and the first five black cadets to be commissioned as pilots of the Army Air Forces were graduated on March 7, 1942.

Cadets were put through a rigorous ground school where they learned meteorology, navigation and instrument training. All phases of flight training from primary through advanced were concentrated at Tuskegee Army Air Field.

10. Major James Ellison, base commander, returns the salute of Mac Ross as he reviews the first class of Tuskegee cadets on the flight line in 1941. *(U.S. Air Force)*

11. A group of aviation cadets report to their instructor at Tuskegee Army Air Field. From left to right: Gabe Hawkins, Henry B. Perry, Richard B. Caesar, unidentified cadet. *(Schomburg Center for Research in Black Culture, N.Y. Public Library)*

10.

11.

12. Aviation cadets at Tuskegee Army Air Field are reviewed by base commander Major James Ellison and his staff. In the background are Vultee BT-13 basic trainers. *(U.S. Air Force)*

13. A flight instructor in the advanced program at Tuskegee briefs primary instructors before a long-distance training flight. *(U.S. Air Force)*

14. Tuskegee Army Air Field cadets are pictured at a formal assembly. *(William R. Thompson)*

15. The first group of black cadets to earn their wings at Tuskegee Army Air Field gathers alongside a Vultee BT-13 trainer. Left to right: Lemuel R. Custis, Mac Ross, Benjamin O. Davis, Jr., George S. Roberts and Charles H. DeBow. *(U.S. Air Force)*

15.

13.

14.

C. ALFRED ANDERSON

Charles Alfred Anderson, known affectionately as "Chief" Anderson, trained many cadets during the primary phase of flight training at Tuskegee Army Air Field. Among his students was the future Air Force general, Daniel "Chappie" James.

Before coming to Tuskegee as a Civilian Pilot Training Program instructor in 1941, Chief Anderson had established a reputation for long-distance flying. Teamed with Dr. Albert E. Forsythe, Anderson made a round trip coast-to-coast flight of the United States in 1933 and the first flight by a land plane from Miami to Nassau in 1934.

16.

18.

16. Anderson was one of a handful of black pilots to have earned a commercial rating in the early 1930s. By the time he arrived at Tuskegee, he had logged over 3,500 hours in the air. *(C. Alfred Anderson)*

17. Anderson *(second from right)* poses with a group of advanced CPT students in 1940. *(Elmer D. Jones)*

18. Anderson *(center)* takes a few moments to relax between flights. He is flanked by Milton P. Crenshaw *(left)* and John S. Perry. *(Elmer D. Jones)*

19.

19. As First Lady, Eleanor Roosevelt did much to promote the cause of equal opportunity for black Americans. She took a special interest in the Tuskegee flight program and, on a visit to the flying school, joined Chief Anderson for an airplane ride around the facility. This event had considerable symbolic value for the entire program of black aviation. *(C. Alfred Anderson)*

17.

20. Two officials of Tuskegee Institute visit armament, engineering and communications trainees at Chanute Field in 1942. Left to right: William R. Thompson, Nelson S. Brooks, Elmer D. Jones, James L. Johnson, George L. Washington (Director, Division of Aeronautics, Tuskegee Institute), Dudley W. Stevenson, Dr. Fred L. Patterson (President, Tuskegee Institute), William D. Townes. (Elmer D. Jones)

21. Two Tuskegee Army Air Field flight instructors, Philip Lee (left) and Roscoe Draper, are seen in front of their Vultee BT-13 trainer. (James O. Plinton, Jr.)

21.

22. The flight instructor staff of Tuskegee Army Air Field poses for a group photograph late in the war. (Perry H. Young, Jr.)

20.

22.

NOEL F. PARRISH

Lieutenant Colonel Noel F. Parrish, base commander at Tuskegee from 1942 to 1946, worked diligently to alleviate the harsh impact of segregation practices within the Army Air Forces. During his tenure, Parrish reversed the pattern of low morale which had developed under earlier commanders. His effective wartime leadership contributed to the ultimate success of the Tuskegee flight training program.

24.

23. Parrish *(front row, fourth from left)* appears with a group of flight instructors at Tuskegee Army Air Field. *(Elmer D. Jones)*

24. Lieutenant Colonel Noel F. Parrish. *(Noel F. Parrish)*

25. Parrish quickly established a rapport with his black officers at Tuskegee Army Air Field. *(Schomburg Center for Research in Black Culture, N.Y. Public Library)*

25.

In Support of Tuskegee Army Air Field

As training of black pilots and technicians grew to meet the demands of the war, additional facilities were required. Pilots of the 332d Fighter Group completed preparations for Mediterranean operations at Selfridge Field, Michigan. The 477th Bombardment Group began training at Selfridge but was later moved to Godman Field, Kentucky, and Freeman Field, Indiana, then sent back to Godman. Air crewmen for the 477th Bombardment Group were trained at Hondo Field and Midland Field, Texas, and Mather Field, California. Aircraft technicians were trained at Chanute Field, Illinois.

26.

26. Armorers of the 332d Fighter Group carry .50 caliber ammunition belts at Selfridge Field, Michigan. The training of skilled ground support personnel became a high priority during the war. *(U.S. Air Force)*

27. Members of the February 1945 graduating class of navigators at Hondo Field, Texas, pose for a group photograph alongside a Beech AT-7 trainer. *(Schomburg Center for Research in Black Culture, N.Y. Public Library)*

28. The men of the 332d Fighter Group prepare for overseas deployment at Selfridge Field, Michigan, in late 1943. *(Elwood T. Driver)*

27.

28.

477TH BOMBARDMENT GROUP

Activated in 1943, the 477th Bombardment Group, made up of the 616th, 617th, 618th and 619th Bombardment Squadrons, trained in a difficult context of racial segregation, low morale, relocations from air base to air base and opposition from the Army Air Forces command. The war ended in 1945 before the 477th reached a war zone.

29.

29. In April 1945, a five-man B-25 crew of the 477th Bombardment Group consults on a flight plan before departing on a training mission. *(Joseph Hardy)*

30. Lieutenant A. A. Rayner, Jr., 616th Bombardment Squadron, and his crew pose in front of their B-25 at Godman Field, Kentucky. Kneeling, left to right: James C. McClain, David L. Glenn, Samuel R. Davis. Standing, left to right: Rayner, Samuel R. Hunter, Edward R. Gibson. *(Joseph Hardy)*

31. A North American B-25 of the 619th Bombardment Squadron on a training flight. *(Joseph Hardy)*

30.

31.

32. Armament technicians of the 619th Bombardment Squadron load a bomb carrier at Godman Field, Kentucky, in 1944. *(Joseph Hardy)*

33.

32.

33. Maintenance technicians of the 477th Bombardment Group prepare a B-25 for a training flight in 1944. *(Joseph Hardy)*

34.

34. A 618th Bombardment Squadron armament technician loads a practice bomb into the bay of a B-25. *(Joseph Hardy)*

35. A 616th Bombardment Squadron waist gunner takes part in a high-altitude training mission. *(Joseph Hardy)*

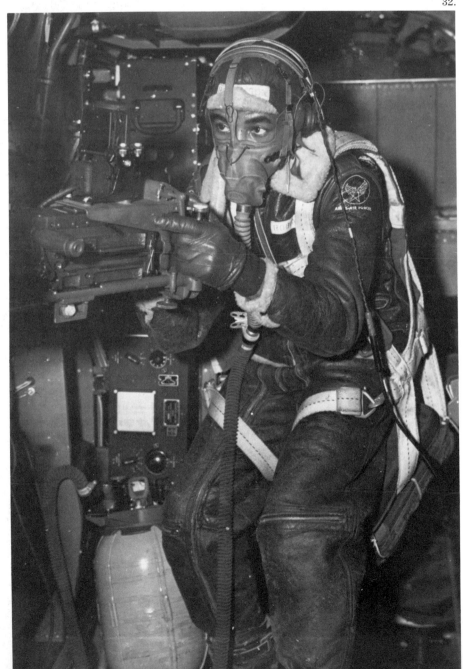

35.

36.

37.

38.

36. A 617th Bombardment Squadron crew chief tests the port engine of a B-25. *(Joseph Hardy)*

37. Members of the 619th Bombardment Squadron make repairs on an airborne camera in 1944. *(Joseph Hardy)*

38. Armament technicians of the 619th Bombardment Squadron mount a .50 caliber machine gun on a B-25. *(Joseph Hardy)*

WINGS FOR WAR

On the eve of World War II, the Army Air Corps mirrored the racial discrimination of the time by barring blacks from flight training. Blacks had volunteered for military service throughout American history—from George Washington's Continental Army to World War I. The long tradition of segregation in the armed services had restricted blacks to four regular U.S. Army units. Elsewhere in the armed forces, blacks were routinely assigned tasks as cooks, drivers and unskilled laborers. Racial exclusion extended as well to base facilities such as exchanges, recreational clubs, theaters and canteens.

To open military service to blacks as pilots, the Air Corps activated the 99th Fighter Squadron in March 1941. The all-black air unit trained at the Tuskegee Army Air Field in Alabama. When the first class of pilots graduated a year later, the United States had entered World War II.

The 99th Fighter Squadron reached the combat zone in North Africa in 1943. Three additional black air units, the 100th, 301st, and 302d Fighter Squadrons, joined the 99th in Italy the following year to form the 332d Fighter Group.

During the war, the black fighter squadrons participated in Allied campaigns in North Africa, Sicily and Italy. The 332d Fighter Group, known as the "Red Tails" because of the distinctive tail markings on their aircraft, flew bomber escort missions for the Fifteenth Air Force, strafed enemy positions in support of the ground forces and engaged in air combat as far north as Berlin.

For black air personnel in World War II, there was a contradiction between fighting for democracy overseas while facing the persistent denial of civil rights at home. Participation in the war effort brought a new sense of pride, an expanded base for black involvement in aviation and a renewed call for an end to segregation in the armed forces.

1. A ground crewman closes the canopy on Major William T. Mattison's P-51C Mustang before a combat mission. (*U.S. Air Force*)

Into Combat

The 99th Fighter Squadron boarded a troopship for North Africa on April 15, 1943, and arrived at Casablanca the morning of April 24. Two years had passed since the activation of the Army Air Corps' first all-black air unit. Under the command of Lieutenant Colonel Benjamin O. Davis, Jr., the 99th—now equipped with P-40 fighters—moved to Cap Bon, Tunisia, as part of the 33d Fighter Group.

The 99th flew its first combat sortie over Pantelleria, an island near Sicily, on June 2, 1943. One month later, Lieutenant Charles B. Hall scored the squadron's first air victory by downing a Focke-Wulf Fw 190.

The transition to combat did not proceed without difficulty. As with all new fighter squadrons, there was the arduous task of learning the ropes—the baptism of fire in a combat zone. Each man faced the challenge of air combat and the squadron had to learn the requirements of coordination with other units. Not all air personnel in the North African theater of combat welcomed the segregated black squadron. Criticism arose even as the 99th adapted to the rigors of war. Despite an awkward debut, black airmen soon earned their place through solid achievement.

When the 99th joined with three other black fighter squadrons to form the 332d Fighter Group in July 1944, black airmen assumed an expanded role in the war. As a component of both the Twelfth and Fifteenth Air Forces, black military pilots flew more than 15,000 sorties and destroyed 261 enemy aircraft.

2.

2. Graham Smith and Elmer D. Jones on the deck of the *Mariposa* enroute to Casablanca, Morocco, in April 1943. *(Elmer D. Jones)*

3. Fighter pilots of the 99th Fighter Squadron just before their assignment to the combat zone in North Africa in 1943. Bottom row, left to right: Charles B. Hall, George R. Bolling, H. V. Clark; center: Paul G. Mitchell, Spann Watson, Willie Ashley, Louis R. Purnell, Erwin B. Lawrence; top: Allen Lane, Graham Smith, William A. Campbell, Faith McGinnis. *(Elmer D. Jones)*

4. P-40s of the 99th Fighter Squadron are deployed at the forward air base at Cap Bon, Tunisia, in June 1943. *(Elmer D. Jones)*

3.

4.

5. In North Africa in 1942, Lieutenant Colonel Benjamin O. Davis, Jr., Commander of the 99th Fighter Squadron, stands beside his P-40 "Agita Jo." *(Benjamin O. Davis, Jr.)*

6. Lieutenant James B. Knighten in the cockpit of his P-40 "Eel II" at Licata, Sicily, in October 1943. *(William R. Thompson)*

7. On a hot July day in 1943, Lieutenant Sidney Brooks stands next to his P-40 fighter, "El Cid." Brooks was killed in action over Sicily later that summer. *(Elmer D. Jones)*

7.

10. Lieutenant Willie H. Fuller poses next to his P-40 fighter "Ruthea" during the Sicilian campaign. Interlocking steel mats were laid out to make an improvised airstrip. Extremes of weather—heat, rain and mud—were constant adversaries. *(William R. Thompson)*

8.

8. Captain Elmer D. Jones, commanding officer of the service group attached to the 99th Fighter Squadron, stands next to one of the P-39 Airacobras used for harbor patrol over the Bay of Naples. *(Elmer D. Jones)*

9. P-40s of the 99th Fighter Squadron take off from their base at Licata, Sicily, in 1943. *(William R. Thompson)*

11.

11. Lieutenant Spann Watson in the cockpit of his P-40 fighter at Cap Bon, Tunisia. *(Schomburg Center for Research in Black Culture, N.Y. Public Library)*

10.

9.

The 99th Fighter Squadron's First Victory

Charles B. Hall of Brazil, Indiana, became the first black fighter pilot to down an enemy aircraft on July 21, 1943. While escorting B-25 bombers over Italy on his eighth mission, Hall spotted two Focke-Wulf Fw 190s approaching after the bombers had dropped their bombs on the enemy-held Castelvetrano airfield. He quickly maneuvered into the space between the bombers and fighters and turned inside the Fw 190s. Hall fired a long burst at one of the Fw 190s as it turned left. After several hits, the aircraft fell off and crashed into the ground.

The squadron's important benchmark of success occurred against a backdrop of sadness. On the same day that Charles Hall scored his memorable victory, the 99th lost two of its pilots—Sherman White and James McCullin.

Hall earned the respect of his squadron mates with his boldness and flying skill. Before he ended his combat tour—flying P-40s—Hall downed a total of three enemy aircraft.

13.

13. Charles B. Hall. *(Benjamin O. Davis, Jr.)*

CHARLES HALL'S VICTORY CELEBRATION

Louis R. Purnell, one of the original members of the 99th Fighter Squadron, describes how the squadron rewarded Charles Hall for his air victory:

"Although Charlie Hall was awarded the Distinguished Flying Cross for being the first black to shoot down a German aircraft, his most appreciated prize may well have been an ice-cold bottle of Coca Cola.

"While moving our P-40 aircraft up to the battle zone, one of several overnight stops was the Maison Blanche Air Base at Tunis, Tunisia. It was there that I obtained a bottle of America's leading soft drink. Upon arrival at our base, I deposited the precious bottle in our squadron safe.

"The day of Charlie's victory we obtained a block of ice from a town that was 15 miles from our base. We chilled the bottle of Coke in a one-gallon fruit juice can packed with ice. It was in the shade of a grove of olive trees that the bottle of Coke—probably the only one in the Mediterranean Theater of Operations—came to a well-deserved end."

12.

12. Hall poses for the camera with his coveted bottle of Coke. *(Elmer D. Jones)*

14. Lieutenant Colonel Benjamin O. Davis, Jr. describes the combat sortie in which Charles Hall scored his first victory. *(Benjamin O. Davis, Jr.)*

15. Hall *(center)* chats with squadron mates Willie Fuller *(left)* and James T. Wiley after his celebrated victory. *(Elmer D. Jones)*

14.

15.

BENJAMIN O. DAVIS, JR. CALLED HOME

In late August 1943, Lieutenant Colonel Benjamin O. Davis, Jr. received orders to return home to take command of the all-black 332d Fighter Group. The new group consisted of the 100th, 301st and 302d Fighter Squadrons. The air unit had been activated on October 13, 1942, at Tuskegee, but the center for training shifted to Selfridge Field, Michigan, to meet the requirements for the expanded Army Air Forces program for black pilots. The 332d Fighter Group arrived in Italy in February 1944.

16. Colonel Davis bids farewell to the 99th Fighter Squadron at Licata, Sicily, in August 1943. During his command, the 99th participated in the Pantelleria and Sicilian campaigns, conducted numerous strafing and bomber escort missions for the Twelfth Air Force, and for a brief time flew air support for the British Eighth Army under General Bernard Montgomery. *(Benjamin O. Davis, Jr.)*

16.

17.

17. Major George S. "Spanky" Roberts. *(William R. Thompson)*

18. Major Roberts in the cockpit of his P-51C in Italy, 1944. *(William R. Thompson)*

18.

GEORGE S. "SPANKY" ROBERTS

Major George S. Roberts assumed command of the 99th Fighter Squadron in August 1943. A popular and effective successor to Colonel Davis, "Spanky" Roberts led the 99th during the winter of 1943-1944 when the squadron gained valued combat experience as part of the 79th Fighter Group. At Anzio in January and February of 1944, the 99th displayed aggressiveness and skill in support of the Allied landings. Roberts returned to the United States after completing 78 missions. Much of the confidence and high morale of the 99th in 1944 stemmed from Major Roberts' leadership as squadron commander.

Italian Campaign, 1944-1945

THE 332D FIGHTER GROUP

When the three squadrons of the 332d Fighter Group reached the Italian combat zone in February 1944, they flew P-39 Airacobras. Later they transferred briefly to P-47 Thunderbolts which were painted with the distinctive red tail markings of the unit. By July 1944, the 332d—now enlarged to include the veteran 99th Fighter Squadron—had made the transition to P-51 Mustangs at Ramitelli, Italy. The four-squadron fighter group performed a diverse role for the remainder of the war —attacking enemy installations and troop concentrations, engaging in air combat in the skies of northern Italy, and providing effective escort for American bombers over central and eastern Europe.

19.

19. Colonel Benjamin O. Davis, Jr., shown in the cockpit of his P-51 Mustang, returned to Italy on January 29, 1944, as Commander of the 332d Fighter Group. *(Benjamin O. Davis, Jr.)*

20.

20. P-51 Mustangs of the 332d Fighter Group prepare to take off from their base at Ramitelli, Italy, for a bomber escort mission. *(William R. Thompson)*

21.

21. Intelligence Officer Cornelius Vincent *(center)* briefs pilots of the 99th Fighter Squadron before a combat mission. *(William R. Thompson)*

22. Officers of the 332d Fighter Group. Bottom row, left to right: Edward C. Gleed, Nelson Brooks, Benjamin O. Davis, Jr., unidentified officer, George S. Roberts, Thomas J. Money; top: Denzal Harvey, Cyrus W. Perry, Ray B. Ware. *(Benjamin O. Davis, Jr.)*

23. On the occasion of the 200th mission of the 332d Fighter Group, Colonel Benjamin O. Davis, Jr. briefs pilots at Ramitelli. *(U.S. Air Force)*

23.

22.

24.

25.

27.

24. Lieutenants Lee Rayford, John W. Rogers and Spann Watson of the 332d Fighter Group relax along the flight line in 1944. *(Elmer D. Jones)*

25. Lieutenant Edward Thomas prepares to depart for a mission in 1944. Thomas survived the war but was killed in an aircraft accident at Tuskegee Army Air Field in May 1946. *(William R. Thompson)*

26. Sitting on the wing of the P-51C "Rattlesnake," a crew chief gives directions to the pilot as he taxis his aircraft to the runway in August 1944. *(U.S. Air Force)*

27. Lieutenants Andrew D. Turner and C. D. Lester discuss an air battle over Italy in 1944. Turner completed 69 combat missions and was awarded the Distinguished Flying Cross. While serving as Operations and Training Officer for the 332d Fighter Wing, Turner lost his life in a midair collision in 1947. *(U.S. Air Force)*

26.

28. Lieutenant Wendell O. Pruitt *(right)* is greeted by fellow pilot John F. Briggs. Pruitt received the Distinguished Flying Cross for gallantry in a strafing attack on enemy shipping in June 1944. *(U.S. Air Force)*

29. Lieutenant Lee A. Archer, a native of New York City, became one of the most proficient fighter pilots in the 332d Fighter Group. *(U.S. Air Force)*

30. Lieutenant Elwood T. Driver jokes for the camera at Licata, Sicily. Driver flew as a replacement pilot with the 99th Fighter Squadron. *(William R. Thompson)*

31. A 99th Fighter Squadron pilot studies his map before going out on a mission. *(William R. Thompson)*

32. James E. Johnson, head of the sheet metal section for the 332d Fighter Group, paints "Bernice Baby" on a P-51 Mustang. *(U.S. Air Force)*

28.

29.

30.

32.

31.

Ground Crews

Ground crews played a key role in the combat history of the 99th Fighter Squadron and the 332d Fighter Group. Specialists performed repair, maintenance and armament functions under primitive conditions. Their duties became more complicated in 1944, as the Allied forces advanced into Italy. The constant rebasing of air operations became necessary in order for the 332d to keep pace with the advancing front lines.

33.

33. John T. Fields, an armament technician of the 332d Fighter Group, loads a P-51 Mustang with .50 caliber ammunition. (*U.S. Air Force*)

34. Having removed a .50 caliber machine gun from a P-51 Mustang, an armorer carries the weapon to a work station for routine inspection during the Italian campaign in 1944. (*U.S. Air Force*)

35. Staff/Sergeant Bill Hall (*left*), crew chief, leads the effort to complete routine maintenance on a P-40 of the 99th Fighter Squadron. (*William R. Thompson*)

34.

35.

36. With a ground crewman, Lieutenant Elwood T. Driver *(left)* inspects bombs on his P-40 fighter. *(William R. Thompson)*

37. Ground crewmen repair a wing section of a P-51 Mustang. Constant maintenance and repair were necessary to keep the 332d operational, and ground crews quickly earned the respect of the fighter pilots for their expert work. *(Elmer D. Jones)*

37.

38.

38. Two pilots of the 99th Fighter Squadron *(foreground)* look on as members of the ground crew work on a P-40 fighter. *(William R. Thompson)*

39. A typical P-51 of the 332d Fighter Group. The distinctive red tail marking of the unit is evident on this aircraft flown by Elwood T. Driver. *(Elwood T. Driver)*

39.

Visiting Dignitaries

During their combat tour in North Africa, Sicily and Italy, black air units received many visitors from the Army Air Forces and Allied commands. These visits reflected the wartime interest in the Tuskegee airmen.

41.

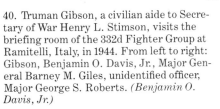

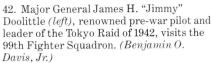

42.

43.

40. Truman Gibson, a civilian aide to Secretary of War Henry L. Stimson, visits the briefing room of the 332d Fighter Group at Ramitelli, Italy, in 1944. From left to right: Gibson, Benjamin O. Davis, Jr., Major General Barney M. Giles, unidentified officer, Major George S. Roberts. *(Benjamin O. Davis, Jr.)*

41. Lieutenant General Carl A. Spaatz, Commander, U.S. Strategic Air Forces *(left)*, visits Colonel Benjamin O. Davis, Jr., in 1944. *(Benjamin O. Davis, Jr.)*

42. Major General James H. "Jimmy" Doolittle *(left)*, renowned pre-war pilot and leader of the Tokyo Raid of 1942, visits the 99th Fighter Squadron. *(Benjamin O. Davis, Jr.)*

43. General Dwight D. Eisenhower, Allied Commander, visits the 99th Fighter Squadron at Cap Bon, Tunisia, in June 1943. General Eisenhower *(left)* is accompanied by Lieutenant General Carl A. Spaatz *(foreground)*, Major General John K. Cannon and Colonel Benjamin O. Davis, Jr. *(Elmer D. Jones)*

40.

Life at the Front

Black air personnel faced predictable challenges at the front. Their experiences were identical to other Allied air units. There were primitive field conditions, muddy airstrips, hard work, boredom and homesickness broken by occasional visits by U.S.O. entertainers.

45.

44.

44. The visit of heavyweight boxing champion Joe Louis *(right)* became a special event. *(William R. Thompson)*

45. Writing home was a high priority for all servicemen. Here, Herbert Carter of the 99th Fighter Squadron writes a letter from the wing of a P-40 fighter. *(William R. Thompson)*

46. A sketch by a black airman of the 332d Fighter Group Headquarters, Ramitelli Air Base, in 1944. *(Benjamin O. Davis, Jr.)*

47. The radio was a prized possession to he shared with all. Here black airmen listen to a broadcast with obvious enthusiasm. *(Elmer D. Jones)*

46.

47.

48.

48. The appearance of entertainer Ella Fitzgerald was a highlight for the airmen of the 99th Fighter Squadron in 1944. *(Elmer D. Jones)*

49. A jazz combo of the 99th Fighter Squadron. *(Elmer D. Jones)*

50. Black airmen gather for a drink and conversation at their rest camp in Naples, Italy. From left to right: Lieutenant Wylie Selden, Captain Fred Hutchinson, unidentified Red Cross worker, Lieutenants George Gray and F. Johnson.

49.

51.

51. An all-black U.S.O. entertainment group arrives to perform for black air personnel in Italy. The leader of the group was Willie Bryant *(top row, fourth from left)*, a popular master of ceremonies at the Apollo Theater in New York City. *(Elmer D. Jones)*

50.

"Lucky" Lester's Account of His Three Victories

Lieutenant C. D. "Lucky" Lester flew his North American P-51 Mustang, "Miss Pelt," to a remarkable three-victory day on July 18, 1944. (52.) Lester earned the Distinguished Flying Cross and went on to fly in the post-war integrated Air Force. (*U.S. Air Force*)

52.

"It was a clear day in July 1944 when the P-51 Mustangs of the 332d Fighter Group took off from their airfield at Ramitelli, Italy. Our mission was to rendezvous over northern Italy's Po Valley at 25,000 feet with B-17 Flying Fortresses enroute to bomb a German airfield in southern Germany. We had been given the task of escorting the bombers to the target and back, providing protection from enemy aircraft. We relished the assignment since it allowed us to conduct a fighter sweep, which meant we provided general cover, but had no specific group of 'Forts' to protect. I flew with the 100th Fighter Squadron. The name 'Lucky' stuck because of all the tight situations from which I had escaped without a scratch or even a bullet hole in my aircraft.

"The rendezvous was made on time at 25,000 feet. The bombers always came in higher than planned and continued to climb so that they reached the target well over 30,000 feet (the higher, the safer from ground fire). The other squadrons of the 332d began their close

cover at 27,000 feet. We were around 29,000 feet when bogeys (enemy aircraft) were spotted above us.

"We were flying a loose combat formation, 200 feet apart and zig-zagging. The flight leader commanded 'hard right turn and punch tanks' (drop external fuel tanks) when Number Four called that he could not get one of his two tanks off. He was never seen again. At this time, I saw a formation of Messerschmitt Bf 109s straight ahead, but slightly lower; I closed to about 200 feet and started to fire. Smoke began to pour out of the 109 and the aircraft exploded. I was going so fast I was sure I would hit some of the debris from the explosion, but luckily I didn't.

"As I was dodging pieces of aircraft, I saw another 109 to my right, all alone on a heading 90 degrees to mine, but at the same altitude. I turned onto his tail and closed to about 200 feet while firing. His aircraft started to smoke and almost stopped. My closure was so fast I began to overtake him. When I overran him, I looked down to see the enemy pilot

emerge from his burning aircraft. I remember seeing his blonde hair as he bailed out at approximately 8,000 feet.

"By this time I was alone and looking for my flight mates when I spotted the third 109 flying very low, about 1,000 feet off the ground. I dove to the right behind him and opened fire. As I scored hits, he apparently thought he had enough altitude to use a 'split-S' maneuver to evade me (A 'split-S' is a one-half loop going down; the aircraft is rolled upside down and pulled straight through until it is right side up—not recommended below 3,500 feet).

"We were approximately 1,000 feet above the ground and, as I did a diving turn, I saw the 109 go straight into the ground. During the return flight, it took a while to realize how much had happened in that brief span of time (4-6 minutes maximum). Everything went the same as in training except for the real bullets. *Real Bullets!!!* Until then the danger of this mission had never occurred to me."

49

332d Fighter Group

99th Fighter Squadron

100th Fighter Squadron

301st Fighter Squadron

302d Fighter Squadron

53. "Two Down, One to Go." Oil.
William S. Phillips. 1982.

C. D. "Lucky" Lester scores his second of
three victories on July 18, 1944.

332d Fighter Pilots in Action

While flying sorties over Italy, Germany and Eastern Europe, the Red Tails scored many victories. There were also risks and, on occasion, losses to enemy action. As with other Allied air units, the 332d Fighter Group accepted the dangers of combat and made the necessary sacrifices for the war effort.

54.

54. Lieutenant Andrew D. Marshall narrowly avoided death over Greece when enemy anti-aircraft fire destroyed his fighter. Marshall escaped from his burning aircraft with minor cuts and bruises. He was later rescued by Greek partisans. *(U.S. Air Force)*

55. Not all fighter pilots escaped death in the performance of their duty. Pictured here is Captain Erwin B. Lawrence of Cleveland, Ohio, who lost his life in a strafing attack on an enemy airfield in Germany. Lawrence was part of the original 99th Fighter Squadron and succeeded Major George S. "Spanky" Roberts as squadron commander in April 1944. *(William R. Thompson)*

56. Captain A. G. McDaniel inspects the damage to his P-51 Mustang as a result of enemy fire over the Danube River. From left to right: Sergeant Richard Adams, McDaniel, Lieutenants James McFatridge and Ulysses Taylor. *(U.S. Air Force)*

55.

56.

Bomber Escort

The 332d Fighter Group established a solid record of achievement. During the latter stages of the war, the unit performed the important task of bomber escort in support of the Fifteenth Air Force. Members of the 332d Fighter Group took pride in the fact that they never lost a bomber to enemy fighters.

57. P-51 Mustang "7" joins fighters from the Fifteenth Air Force in a flight over Yugoslavia. (*U.S. Air Force*)

58. Red Tail P-51 "Jim" lands after a bomber escort mission. *(Benjamin O. Davis, Jr.)*

59. To perform their crucial task of protecting bombers, P-51s of the 332d Fighter Group were fitted with external fuel tanks to allow for maximum long-distance escort duty. Here ground crewmen install an external tank. *(U.S. Air Force)*

59.

60. Black airmen stand beside a B-24 bomber of the Fifteenth Air Force. One of the primary tasks of the 332d Fighter Group was to protect Allied bombing missions over central and eastern Europe. *(U.S. Air Force)*

58.

60.

Distinguished Unit Citation

The 332d Fighter Group earned the Distinguished Unit Citation for "outstanding performance and extraordinary heroism" while flying an escort mission to Berlin on March 24, 1945.

61. Colonel Benjamin O. Davis, Jr. sits in the cockpit of his P-51 fighter as he talks to officers in charge of ground crews. *(William R. Thompson)*

ERA OF CHANGE

While the 332d Fighter Group was piling up a record of successes in the war overseas, the 477th Bombardment Group faced its share of frustrations and failures at home. From 1943, when the 477th was activated, to the end of the war, low morale, caused by transfers from base to base and the rigidly-segregated atmosphere of a stateside training situation, impeded the organization's effectiveness.

There were also racial protests. The worst of these, the so-called Freeman Field mutiny of April 1945, erupted over the question of whether black officers of the 477th had the right to use the officers' club on base. As a result of the Freeman Field protest, General Henry H. "Hap" Arnold replaced the existing command structure of white officers with blacks and placed them under the leadership of Colonel Benjamin O. Davis, Jr.

In 1945, elements of the returning 332d Fighter Group joined the 477th to form the 477th Composite Group which later became the 332d Fighter Wing. From the end of the war until mid-1949, Colonel Davis commanded the segregated black air units. Under his leadership, morale improved and the group performed well.

The Air Force soon realized that a segregated force was wasteful and inefficient and took steps to integrate. Agreeing that a segregated military service should be eliminated, President Harry S Truman on July 26, 1948, signed Executive Order 9981 which signaled the abandonment of the official policy of segregation in the armed forces.

In the Korean and Vietnam wars, significant numbers of black Air Force pilots and crew members were routinely integrated into military aviation and assigned to combat units with their white counterparts. Although the Air Force set the pace for the integration of blacks into all levels of management and operations, the Army, Navy and Marine Corps also provided career opportunities in aviation.

Black gains in military aviation, along with the equal rights legislation of the 1960s and the affirmative action programs of the 1970s, opened up opportunities in other areas such as general and commercial aviation and the space program. By the 1980s, four black astronauts had been assigned to the Space Shuttle program and blacks were finding greater opportunities in the aerospace community.

1. The Space Shuttle *Challenger* lifts off in the pre-dawn darkness from Kennedy Space Center, Florida, on August 30, 1983. On this mission, STS-8, Guion S. Bluford, Jr. (top right) became the first black astronaut in space. (NASA)

477th Composite Group

Under the command of Colonel Benjamin O. Davis, Jr., the 477th Composite Group (later the 332d Fighter Wing) performed admirably, passing an Operational Readiness Inspection and winning an Air Force gunnery meet in May 1949. The B-25 pilots of the old 477th Bombardment Group were retrained to become fighter pilots and the unit participated in Tactical Air Command war games and maneuvers. The segregated situation of these men was not only indefensible but also inefficient, and plans were made to integrate them into the Air Force.

2. Colonel Benjamin O. Davis, Jr. *(far left)*, post-war commander of the 477th Composite Group, confers with his officers in 1946. Davis was the first black to command an Air Force base in the United States. *(Benjamin O. Davis, Jr.)*

3. Republic P-47N Thunderbolts of the all-black 332d Fighter Wing at Lockbourne Air Force Base, Ohio. In a little over three months in 1946, the 477th Composite Group underwent two reorganizations to emerge as the 332d Fighter Wing. *(Benjamin O. Davis, Jr.)*

2.

3.

4. A 477th Composite Group maintenance crew prepares an engine for overhaul. *(Benjamin O. Davis, Jr.)*

5. Lieutenant Floyd Thompson, 332d Fighter Wing, gazes pensively from the cockpit of his Republic P-47N. *(Benjamin O. Davis, Jr.)*

6. A 332d Fighter Wing P-47N returns from maneuvers at Lockbourne Air Force Base, Ohio. *(Benjamin O. Davis, Jr.)*

4.

5.

6.

President Truman and the Fahy Committee

Executive Order 9981 endorsed equality of treatment and opportunity for all members of the military, established the Fahy Committee (President's Committee on Equality of Treatment in the Armed Services) to carry out its provisions, and helped to open the door for the eventual integration of blacks into a variety of military roles.

7. The Fahy Committee meets with President Harry S Truman in January 1949. Seated from left to right: Secretary of Defense James V. Forrestal, President Truman, and Alphonsus J. Donahue. Standing from left to right: John H. Sengstacke, William E. Stevenson, Secretary of the Army Kenneth C. Royall, Secretary of the Air Force W. Stuart Symington, Lester B. Granger, Dwight R. G. Palmer, Secretary of the Navy John L. Sullivan and committee chairman Charles Fahy. (*U.S. Air Force*)

7.

Contemporary Military Aviation

Military aviation was the avenue through which many blacks were assimilated into the aeronautical community. Having proved their ability to fly in combat during World War II, blacks found increased opportunities for making military aviation a profession during the Korean and Vietnam wars. By the mid-1970s, blacks had gained membership in the select USAF Demonstration Squadron, the Thunderbirds.

8. Lieutenant William E. Brown, Jr. is seen here alongside his North American F-86 Sabre in Korea in March 1953. Later promoted to Major General, Brown has had an outstanding career which includes 125 combat missions in the Korean War and 100 missions in Southeast Asia during the Vietnam War. *(U.S. Air Force)*

8.

Ensign Jesse L. Brown was the first black naval aviator. While flying a close air support mission in the Korean War, Ensign Brown's plane was struck by fire from an enemy aircraft. A fellow pilot, Lieutenant Thomas J. Hudner, made a dangerous landing in mountainous terrain and under severe weather conditions to free Brown from the wreckage of his aircraft, but the attempt was unsuccessful. Brown was posthumously awarded the Distinguished Flying Cross, Air Medal, and Purple Heart. Hudner was awarded the Medal of Honor for attempting to save Ensign Brown's life.

9. Ensign Jesse L. Brown looks out from the cockpit of his Grumman F8F Bearcat fighter. (U.S. Navy)

10. Ensign Brown enjoys a few leisure moments with a fellow officer on board the USS Leyte. (U.S. Navy)

11. At a commissioning ceremony for the escort ship USS Jesse L. Brown in 1973, Captain Thomas J. Hudner (left) stands with Jesse Brown's widow, Mrs. Gilbert Thorne, and Rear Admiral Samuel L. Gravely, Jr. (U.S. Navy)

9.

10.

11.

12.

12. At a small outpost in Qui Nhon, Vietnam, Air Force pilots of the 34th Tactical Group plan a Douglas A1E strike against the Viet Cong. From left to right: Captain James T. Harwood, First Lieutenant James H. Manly and Captain Robert H. Tice. *(U.S. Air Force)*

13. During a March 1968 rescue mission in South Vietnam, an HH-43F helicopter crew of the 38th Aerospace Rescue and Recovery Squadron, U.S. Air Force, assists a wounded U.S. Navy Patrol Boat crewman. Left to right: Captain Leslie E. Johnson, co-pilot, Airman First Class Archelous Whitehead, Jr. and Airman First Class Larry D. Nickolson. *(U.S. Air Force)*

14. Air Force F-4C Phantom pilots Captain Everett T. Raspberry *(left)* and Lieutenant Robert W. Western after a successful MiG-hunt over North Vietnam in January 1967. *(U.S. Air Force)*

13.

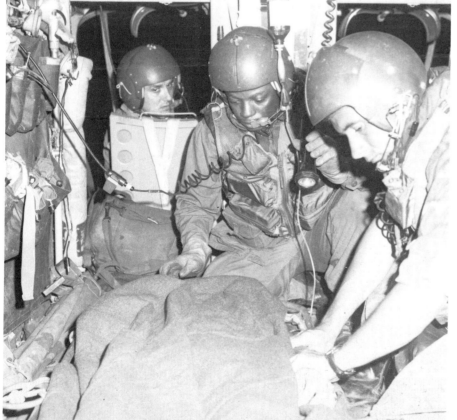

14.

15. At Clark Air Force Base in the Philippines, Air Force Colonel Fred V. Cherry, a recently released prisoner of war in North Vietnam, gets a light from Lieutenant Colonel James Warren. Cherry was held captive for more than seven years. *(U.S. Air Force.*

63

15.

General Daniel "Chappie" James, Jr. was America's first black four-star general. A combat veteran of the Korean and Vietnam wars, James flew many wartime missions and held a variety of leadership positions until his death in 1978.

16.

16. Colonel James in a discussion with President Lyndon B. Johnson in 1970. *(U.S. Air Force)*

17. James is shown in front of his McDonnell-Douglas F-4C Phantom in Thailand during the Vietnam War. While assigned to the 8th Tactical Fighter Wing, he flew 78 combat missions over Vietnam. *(U.S. Air Force)*

18. General James at a press conference in 1975, shortly after he had been named Commander-in-Chief of the North American Air Defense Command and awarded his fourth star. *(U.S. Air Force)*

18.

17.

19.

20.

21.

19. Frank E. Petersen, Jr. is a combat veteran of Korea and Vietnam. In 1968 he became the first black officer to command a squadron in either the U.S. Navy or Marine Corps. Petersen later advanced to the rank of Brigadier General. (U.S. Marine Corps)

20. Captain Ronald A. Radcliffe, U.S. Army, a helicopter pilot in the Vietnam War, received the coveted Army Aviator of the Year Award in 1972 for repeated acts of heroism. (Army Aviation Association of America)

21. In 1974, Captain Lloyd Newton became the first black pilot to join the elite U.S. Air Force Thunderbirds. (U.S. Air Force)

22.

22. Captain Joseph N. "Pete" Peterson, a veteran of the Thunderbirds, died tragically along with three of his fellow pilots on January 18, 1982, while practicing a difficult line-abreast loop in the Nevada desert. (U.S. Air Force)

23. The U.S. Air Force Thunderbirds. (U.S. Air Force)

23.

BENJAMIN O. DAVIS, JR.

Benjamin O. Davis, Jr., a 1936 graduate of West Point, commanded the 99th Fighter Squadron and later the 332d Fighter Group. During World War II, he earned the Distinguished Flying Cross and the Silver Star for gallantry in a strafing attack on an enemy airfield in Germany.

Davis became the first black general in the U.S. Air Force in 1954. His distinguished military career extended to 1970 and included, among other assignments, command of the Thirteenth Air Force in the Philippines, the United Nations Command in Korea, and, at home, the U.S. Strike Command.

After retirement from the military, Davis held several government posts dealing with public safety, including the campaign to halt hijackings. Davis also served as Assistant Secretary of Transportation for Environment, Safety and Consumer Affairs in the U.S. Department of Transportation.

24.

24. Cadet Benjamin O. Davis, Jr., U.S. Military Academy, class of 1936. While at West Point, Davis endured the prejudice of his fellow cadets by being forced to submit to the "silent treatment," a form of hazing that dictated that no one speak to him. (*Benjamin O. Davis, Jr.*)

25. General Benjamin O. Davis, Sr. pins the Distinguished Flying Cross on his son, Colonel Benjamin O. Davis, Jr., in Italy on May 29, 1944. (*U.S. Air Force*)

26. Brigadier General Benjamin O. Davis, Jr. greets Chiang Kai-shek, Chinese Nationalist leader. During the mid-1950s, Davis was assigned as Vice Commander, Thirteenth Air Force, with additional duty as Commander, Air Task Force 13 (Provisional) on Taipei, Formosa. (*Benjamin O. Davis, Jr.*)

27. Colonel Davis receives a visit from Major General Elwood Quesada at Lockbourne Air Force Base, Ohio, in 1946. (*Benjamin O. Davis, Jr.*)

26.

27.

28.

29.

28. While serving as Commander of the 51st Fighter-Interceptor Wing, Far East Air Forces, Korea, Colonel Davis *(center)* discusses a flight maneuver with two of his officers. *(Benjamin O. Davis, Jr.)*

29. Colonel Davis cradles a Korean child during his assignment as Commander of the 51st Fighter-Interceptor Wing in Korea in the early 1950s. *(Benjamin O. Davis, Jr.)*

30. While serving in Seoul, Korea, as Chief of Staff, United Nations Command, Lieutenant General Davis *(second from right)* signs an agreement in 1965 to commit U. S. and Republic of Korea troops to a joint military exercise. Seated at left is Lieutenant General Chul of the Korean Joint Chiefs of Staff. *(Benjamin O. Davis, Jr.)*

31. An integrated Air Force B-26 crew flew the last combat mission of the Korean War in July 1953. From left to right: Airman Third Class Dennis Judd, Lieutenant Donald Mansfield and Lieutenant Bill Ralston. *(U.S. Air Force)*

General Aviation

Black participation in general aviation after World War II continued to be limited by high costs and racial bias. Despite these limitations, blacks successfully took part in general aviation activities as diverse as sport aviation and aircraft design, small airport operation and flight instruction.

John W. Greene, Jr. received his private pilot's license in June 1929. By 1937, he had earned ratings as both a limited commercial and transport pilot and certification as an aircraft and engine mechanic.

Later, Greene established an aviation mechanics course at Phelps Vocational School in Washington, D. C. At the same time, he worked with a local aviation club to establish an airport at Croom, Maryland.

32. John W. Greene, Jr. steps into the cockpit of his Kinner Sportster. In August 1930, Greene was one of only three blacks to hold a transport rating as a pilot. (*John W. Greene, Jr.*)

33. Greene stands beside an Aeronca 7AC Champion at the Columbia Air Center in Croom, Maryland. The airport facility consisted of eight runways and could accommodate as many as 150 arrivals and departures each hour. (*John W. Greene, Jr.*)

32.

33.

34. Greene's life has been devoted to encouraging young blacks in the pursuit of aviation careers. Here (*seated center*) he discusses model building with a group of youngsters. (*John W. Greene, Jr.*)

34.

Neal Loving overcame racial barriers and a physical disability to become a pilot and designer of innovative experimental aircraft. Loving, who lost both of his legs as a result of a glider accident in 1944, designed and built in the basement of his apartment an all-wood, single-seat midget class airplane known as the Loving WR-1 *Love*.

Since the test flight of the *Love* in 1950, Loving has completed two additional aircraft, the WR-2 and WR-3. Loving's WR-1 is now on display at the Experimental Aircraft Association Air Museum in Hales Corners, Wisconsin.

35.

35. Neal Loving in 1943 with his first airplane, a Waco Model 125. *(Neal Loving)*

36. In 1954, Loving flew his WR-1 from Detroit to Cuba and Jamaica, a distance of 2,200 miles. He is seen here with the aircraft at Teterboro, New Jersey, while enroute to Jamaica. *(Neal Loving)*

36.

37. The Loving WR-3, photographed in flight over Springfield, Ohio, in September 1976, has folding wings and is capable of being driven on the highway. *(Neal Loving)*

37.

Lewis A. Jackson purchased his first airplane in 1932 and learned to fly it at Tri-State Airport in Angola, Indiana. By 1940, he had worked his way through college by barnstorming through the midwest, earned a commercial license with an instructor's rating and joined the Coffey School of Aeronautics in Chicago. During World War II, Jackson served as Director of Training at Tuskegee Institute's Division of Aeronautics, where he oversaw the instruction of both civilian and military pilots.

After the war, he earned both a master's and a doctorate in education and served as President of Central State University in Ohio. During this time he became interested in the development of personal aircraft for private flying. He has designed and built a number of experimental aircraft, many of which are roadable, or capable of being driven on the highway as well as flown.

38. Jackson and his latest experimental aircraft, the Jackson 10, completed in 1981. This aircraft has removable wings and can be towed by an automobile. *(Lewis A. Jackson)*

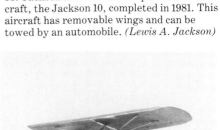

38.

41.

39. Built in the early 1960s, this Jackson aircraft has removable wings and is roadable. *(Lewis A. Jackson)*

40. Another roadable aircraft, built by Jackson in 1975, has been driven a total of over 500 miles. *(Lewis A. Jackson)*

41. The Jackson Versatile I has a cruising speed of 100 mph and can be driven on the highway. *(Lewis A. Jackson)*

40.

Commercial Aviation

Blacks traditionally held blue-collar service jobs as skycaps and ground handlers in the commercial air transport industry, but they were excluded from being pilots or holding key administrative posts. With few exceptions, blacks were unknown in commercial aviation during the post-war years. With the changing social climate of the 1960s, blacks began to make significant strides toward breaking down racial barriers in the airline industry.

Perry H. Young, Jr. learned to fly during the late 1930s, became a flight instructor at the Coffey School of Aeronautics, and served as a civilian flight instructor at Tuskegee Army Air Field during World War II. After the war, Young became a licensed helicopter pilot and in 1956 was hired by New York Airways, a scheduled helicopter airline. After 22 years with New York Airways, Young became chief pilot for New York Helicopter.

42. One of the first blacks to break into commercial aviation, Young is seen here in the cockpit of his New York Airways Vertol 44. The scheduled helicopter airline ferried passengers, cargo and mail between eight suburban airports and a heliport in mid-town Manhattan. *(Perry H. Young, Jr.)*

42.

James O. Plinton, Jr., a pioneer black airline executive, served as a civilian flight instructor at Tuskegee Army Air Field in World War II. After the war, he and a fellow American, Maurice DeYoung, founded Quisqueya Ltd., a Caribbean airline that offered service from Haiti to the Turks and Caicos Islands. From 1957 until his retirement in 1979, Plinton held executive posts with Trans World Airlines and Eastern Air Lines.

43.

43. James O. Plinton, Jr. *(center)* appears in the cockpit of a Stearman PT-13 trainer during his civilian flight instructor days at Tuskegee Army Air Field. At left is cadet "Wilky" Wilkerson. Partially obscured by a strut is cadet Robert Gordon. *(James O. Plinton, Jr.)*

44. James O. Plinton, Jr. *(third from right)* and business partner Maurice DeYoung *(second from left)* gather with dignitaries in front of Quisqueya Ltd.'s Boeing 247D in 1948. Quisqueya was the first airline to serve the Turks and Caicos Islands. *(James O. Plinton, Jr.)*

44.

45. In 1965, Marlon D. Green won a long court battle with Continental Airlines over his right to a job as a commercial pilot. As a result of this important case, blacks began to make significant strides toward breaking down racial barriers in the airline industry. *(Johnson Publishing Co.)*

46. Captain David E. Harris talks about commercial aviation with a group of youngsters. Harris became one of the first black pilots to be employed by a major airline when he joined American Airlines in the mid-1960s. *(David E. Harris)*

45.

46.

The Space Program

The National Aeronautics and Space Administration (NASA) has estimated that for every astronaut, there are nearly 1,000 technical, scientific, and engineering personnel behind the scenes. Increasingly, a larger proportion of these professionals are blacks employed in such areas as aerospace engineering and medicine, astrophysics and the space sciences.

Although progress toward placing a black astronaut in space has been slow, the late 1970s witnessed the first group of black astronauts to be trained for the Space Shuttle program.

50.

47.

47. During John Glenn's historic *Friendship 7* flight in February 1962, Dr. Vance H. Marchbanks, Jr., a black Air Force flight surgeon and former member of the 332d Fighter Group, served on the mission flight control team stationed in Kano, Nigeria. Marchbanks monitored astronaut Glenn's vital signs as Glenn orbited the Earth. Here, Marchbanks pores over medical charts in conjunction with the flight. *(Vance H. Marchbanks, Jr.)*

48. Isaac Gillam IV *(left)*, Special Assistant for Space Transportation Systems at NASA, served as Director of the Dryden Flight Research Center at Edwards Air Force Base, California, where he was also Director of Shuttle Operations. *(NASA)*

49. A promising start toward integrating the astronaut program was made in 1963 when the U.S. Air Force astronaut selection board nominated Captain Edward J. Dwight, Jr. for the manned space flight training program. Dwight was passed over when the final selection was made. Coming amid charges of racial discrimination, Dwight's dismissal was controversial. *(U.S. Air Force)*

50. In 1967, Air Force Major Robert H. Lawrence, Jr. was selected to become an astronaut in the Department of Defense's Manned Orbiting Laboratory Program (MOL). Lawrence, a pilot-scientist with a doctorate in nuclear chemistry, was killed in a tragic aircraft accident later that year. *(U.S. Air Force)*

48.

49.

51.

51. Guion S. Bluford, Jr. holds a doctorate in aerospace engineering from the Air Force Institute of Technology. Before being selected for astronaut training, he was an Air Force fighter pilot in Vietnam with 144 combat missions. (NASA)

52. Mission specialist Bluford participates in a medical test on board the *Challenger* Space Shuttle during the August 30–September 5, 1983 space flight. Bluford helped to deploy the Indian National Satellite, INSAT-1B, from *Challenger*'s cargo bay on the second day of the mission. (NASA)

52.

53. Ronald E. McNair holds a doctorate in physics from the Massachusetts Institute of Technology. Before he began his training as an astronaut, McNair was a staff physicist with Hughes Research Laboratories, where he investigated laser phenomena. *(NASA)*

54. Frederick D. Gregory is a 1964 graduate of the U. S. Air Force Academy and holds a Master of Science degree in information systems from George Washington University. Before his selection as an astronaut, Gregory was an Air Force and NASA test pilot. *(NASA)*

55. Charles F. Bolden is a 1968 graduate of the U. S. Naval Academy and holds a Master of Science degree in systems management from the University of Southern California. Before he became an astronaut, Bolden served as a test pilot at the Naval Air Test Center. *(NASA)*

ACKNOWLEDGMENTS

THE AUTHORS are gratified by the assistance given us by so many people while we were engaged in this project. To C. Alfred Anderson, Cornelius R. Coffey, General Benjamin O. Davis, Jr., and Agatha Davis, Dr. Albert E. Forsythe, Harold Hurd, Elmer D. Jones, William R. Thompson and Ted Robinson, we express our special and everlasting thanks and appreciation for contributions of photographs and documentary material as well as advice and support.

We would also like to thank Don Lopez, Chairman of the Aeronautics Department, National Air and Space Museum, both for his unstinting encouragement and advice and for being a wellspring of creative ideas; Walter Boyne, Director, National Air and Space Museum, for his continued support, and Lou Purnell, Associate Curator, Space Science and Exploration Department, National Air and Space Museum, for his invaluable help on the project.

To the following persons, without whose cooperation and assistance this book would not have been possible, we also express our appreciation: Thomas C. Allen; Janet Bragg; Charles M. Brown; Deborah K. Dawson; Elwood T. Driver; Earl N. Franklin; Mike Gentry, National Aeronautics and Space Administration; Dicey Gibbs; Isaac Gillam IV; Tony Goodstone; John W. Greene, Jr.; Alan L. Gropman; Betty Gubert, Schomburg Center for Research in Black Culture, N.Y. Public Library; Joseph Hardy; David E. Harris; Philip Hart; Reginald C. Hayes, Johnson Publishing Company; Charles Hilty; Arthur H. Kesten; Lewis A. Jackson; Marjorie Kriz; Clarence D. Lester; Neil Loving; Paige Lucas; Dr. Vance H. Marchbanks, Jr.; Effie Matthews; Chere Negaard, Northrop University Library; Debra Newman; Noel F. Parrish; Frank E. Petersen, Jr.; Bill Phillips; James O. Plinton, Jr.; Ahmed A. Rayner; Dr. Earl W. Renfroe; George S. Roberts; Charles N. Smallwood; Chauncey E. Spencer; Harold N. Umbarger, Compton Library, Compton, Cal.; Enoch Waters; Spann Watson; Vivian White, U.S. Air Force Museum; Pendleton Woods; Perry H. Young, Jr.

Finally, we would like to thank all of the National Air and Space Museum staff members who contributed their time and effort to the project, especially, Rita Bobowski, June Chocheles, Dorothy Cochrane, Tom Crouch, Linda DuBro, Holly Haynes, Dale Hrabak, Pat Johnston, Lucius Lomax, Sharon McCoy, Helen McMahon, Claudia Oakes, Efrain Ortiz, Susan Owen, Frank Pietropaoli, Vicki Rosenberg, Natalie Rowland, Jay Spenser, Pete Suthard, Bob van der Linden, Jim Vineyard, Dick Wakefield, Janet Wolfe and Patricia Woodside.

A SELECTIVE BIBLIOGRAPHY
AND RESEARCH GUIDE

Since the amount of research material on blacks in American aviation is surprisingly large, the following bibliography is intended to merely suggest books and articles that pertain to the subject. These works are listed in alphabetical order in the section titled "Books and Periodical Articles Relating to Blacks in Aviation" in Part I.

Part II, "Bibliographic Note," presents in brief narrative form a survey of some of the general reference, research and documentary sources available to the researcher who may be interested in studying particular aspects of the history of blacks in American aviation.

PART I: BOOKS AND ARTICLES RELATING TO BLACKS IN AVIATION

HEADWINDS

Allen, Henry. "To Fly, to Brave the Wing." *Washington Post*, September 26, 1979, p. Blff.

Bunch, Lonnie G., III. "In Search of a Dream: The Flight of Herman Banning and Thomas Allen." Paper prepared for an aviation conference sponsored by the American Culture Association. Available in the general files of the National Air and Space Museum.

Carisella, P. J. and James W. Ryan. *The Black Swallow of Death.* Boston: Marlborough House, 1972.

Kriz, Marjorie. "They Had Another Dream." *FAA World*, January 1980, pp. 2-6.

Patterson, Elois. *Memoirs of the Late Bessie Coleman, Aviatrix.* c. Elois Paterson, 1969.

Powell, William J. *Black Wings.* Los Angeles: Ivan Deach, Jr., 1934.

FLIGHT LINES

Austin, Manning. "The Negro is Flying." *Flying and Popular Aviation*, March 1941, p. 32ff.

"School for Willa." *Time*, September 25, 1939, p. 16.

Strickland, Patricia. *The Putt-Putt Air Force: The Story of the Civilian Pilot Training Program and the War Training Service (1939-1944).* Washington, D.C.: U.S. Department of Transportation, Federal Aviation Administration, Aviation Education Staff [n.d.]. Chapter IX deals with black participation in the Civilian Pilot Training Program.

Watson, Ted. "Colored Aviation as It is in Chicago at Oak Hill's Harlem Airport." *The Pittsburgh Courier*, January 13, 1940, p. 12.

WINGS FOR WAR

Blum, John Morton. *V Was for Victory: Politics and American Culture During World War II.* New York: Harcourt Brace Jovanovich, 1976.

Fomer, Jack D. *Blacks and the Military in American History: A New Perspective.* New York: Praeger, 1974.

Dalfiume, Richard M. *Desegregation of the U.S. Armed Forces: Fighting on Two Fronts, 1939-1953.* Columbia, Missouri: University of Missouri Press, 1969.

Francis, Charles. *The Tuskegee Airmen.* Boston: Bruce Humphries, 1955.

Lee, Ulysses. *United States Army in World War II: The Employment of Negro Troops.* Washington, D.C.: Office of the Chief of Military History, U.S. Army, 1966.

Osur, Alan M. *Blacks in the Army Air Forces During World War II: The Problem of Race Relations.* Washington, D.C.: Office of Air Force History, [1977].

Paszek, Lawrence J. "Negroes and the Air Force, 1939-1949." *Military Affairs*, Spring 1977, pp. 1-10.

Polenberg, Richard. *War and Society: The United States, 1941-1945.* Philadelphia: J. B. Lippincott, 1972.

Rose, Robert A. "Lonely Eagles." [two-part article] *Journal of the American Aviation Historical Society*, Summer 1975, pp. 118-27; Winter 1975, pp. 240-52.

ERA OF CHANGE

"Airline Pioneer." *Ebony*, November 1976, p. 103ff.

"Breakthrough on the Airlines." *Ebony*, November 1965, p. 113ff.

Gropman, Alan L. *The Air Force Integrates, 1945-1964.* Washington; D.C.: Office of Air Force History, 1978.

"Legless Pilot Neal Loving Runs School in Detroit." *Ebony*, November 1965, p. 43ff.

MacGregor, Morris J. *Integration of the Armed Forces, 1940-1965.* Washington, D.C.: Center of Military History, 1981.

Northrup, Herbert R. "The Negro in the Aerospace Industry." Report No. 2 in *The Racial Policies of American Industry.* Philadelphia: Industrial Research Unit, Department of Industry, Wharton School of Finance and Commerce, University of Pennsylvania, 1971.

Northrup, Herbert R. *et al.* "The Negro in the Air Transport Industry." Report No. 23 in *The Racial Policies of American Industry.* Philadelphia: Industrial Research Unit, Department of Industry, Wharton School of Finance and Commerce, University of Pennsylvania, 1971.

Osur, Alan M. "Black-White Relations in the U.S. Military, 1940-1972." *Air University Review*, November-December 1981, pp. 69-77.

PART II: BIBLIOGRAPHIC NOTE

The information contained in the following bibliographic note represents some attempt to provide additional guidance concerning periodical and newspaper articles, photographs, motion pictures, documentary sources and bibliographic material that pertain to blacks in American aviation.

PERIODICAL AND NEWSPAPER ARTICLES

Because of the segregated nature of black aviation during the 1920s, '30s and '40s, coverage in white periodicals is very scanty. Consequently, indexing media such as *Readers' Guide to Periodical Literature* (New York: Wilson, 1905 to date), are of little use except for the war years and the post-war period. Unfortunately, there are no indexes of black periodical literature for the period before 1950, although black publications such as *The Crisis, Opportunity* and the *Journal of Negro History* did cover blacks in the armed forces during World War II.

Researchers interested in articles published in black periodicals after 1950 should consult *Index to Selected Periodicals Received in the Hallie Q. Brown Library* (Boston: G. K. Hall, 1961), which covers articles written between 1950 and 1959, and *Index to Periodical Articles by and About Negroes* (Boston: G. K. Hall, 1971), which covers the years 1960 to 1970. Periodicals such as *Ebony* and *Jet* contain a wealth of information concerning blacks in aviation after 1945.

Newspaper coverage in the white press is also extremely limited. The black press, however, covered the subject in depth and much useful information will be found in the *Pittsburgh Courier, Chicago Defender, Baltimore Afro-American* and *California Eagle* (Los Angeles). Indexes for these papers are often a problem, and extensive research still needs to be done to investigate the scope of coverage in the black press.

PHOTOGRAPHS

Although many historic photographs are still in the hands of private collectors, scattered photographs relating to blacks in aviation exist in collections such as those in the Prints and Photographs Division of the Library of Congress and the Schomburg Center for Research in Black Culture, N.Y. Public Library. The Defense Audio Visual Agency (DAVA), Naval Station Anacostia, Washington, D.C., should be consulted for photographs relating to black military aviation.

In the near future, the National Air and Space Museum, Smithsonian Institution, plans to assimilate photography obtained for the exhibit, "Black Wings," into its archival collections and to make this resource available to scholars and other interested persons.

MOTION PICTURES

A great deal of research needs to be done in this area and indexing is a problem. Nevertheless, an excellent film entitled "Wings for this Man," produced by the U.S. Army Air Forces in 1944, chronicles the Tuskegee airmen during World War II. This film, along with others concerning blacks in the U.S. Air Force produced in the "Air Force Now" series, is available from the U.S. Air Force Central Audiovisual Depository, Norton Air Force Base, California.

DOCUMENTARY SOURCES

An extensive collection of unit histories, professional studies and special reports relating to blacks in the Air Force during and after World War II can be found in the Albert F. Simpson Historical Research Center, Maxwell Air Force Base, Alabama.

Documentation concerning the President's Committee on Equality of Treatment in the Armed Services (Fahy Committee) will be found in the Harry S Truman Library, Independence, Missouri. Material on the integration of the U.S. Air Force is contained in various record groups in the collections of the National Archives, Washington, D.C.

BIBLIOGRAPHY

Although very little in the way of published bibliographic information on blacks in aviation exists, R. Ancil Potter's "A Bibliography on Minority Contributions to United States Aviation" (Washington, D.C.: U.S. Department of Transportation, Federal Aviation Administration, 1971) is a good start for researchers interested in broad coverage. Much useful information will also be found in the bibliographies and bibliographic essays which accompany many of the titles listed in Part I. See especially, Alan M. Osur's *Blacks in the Army Air Forces During World War II* and Alan L. Gropman's *The Air Force Integrates*.

MISCELLANY

Since very little is known about the history of black participation in aviation in California during the 1920s and 1930s, William J. Powell's *Craftsmen Aero News* is of particular interest. Published briefly in 1937, *Craftsmen*, the trade journal of Powell's organization, Craftsmen of Black Wings, reflects Powell's firm belief that aviation offered limitless opportunities for black enterprise, especially in Los Angeles, scene of the burgeoning American aircraft industry. A bound copy of *Craftsmen* may be found in the collection of the Schomburg Center for Research in Black Culture, N.Y. Public Library.